The FilmFour
Book of Film Quotes

FILM FOUR 4

First published 2000 by FilmFour Books
an imprint of Macmillan Publishers Ltd
25 Eccleston Place, London SW1W 9NF
Basingstoke and Oxford

www.macmillan.co.uk

Associated companies throughout the world

ISBN 0 7522 7157 1

9 8 7 6 5 4 3 2 1

A CIP catalogue record for this book is available from the British Library.

Quotes selected and compiled by Charlie Carman

Designed by Blackjacks

Printed in Great Britain by The Bath Press

Photograph Acknowledgements: pp3, 6, 7, 9, 10, 11, 12-13, 14, 15, 18-19, 20, 21, 23,
24-25, 26, 27, 28, 29, 30, 31, 32-33, 34, 35, 36, 37, 40, 41, 42, 43, 44-45, 46, 47, 48, 49, 50,
51, 52, 53, 54, 56-57, 60-61, 62, 64: Moviestore Collection. pp4-5, 55: New Line; pp8, 63:
Paramount; p17: Warner Bros; p22: 20th Century Fox; pp38-39: Miramax/Buena Vista;
p59: Handmade Films; p58: Lucasfilm (all courtesy Kobal). p16: © 1964 United Artists.

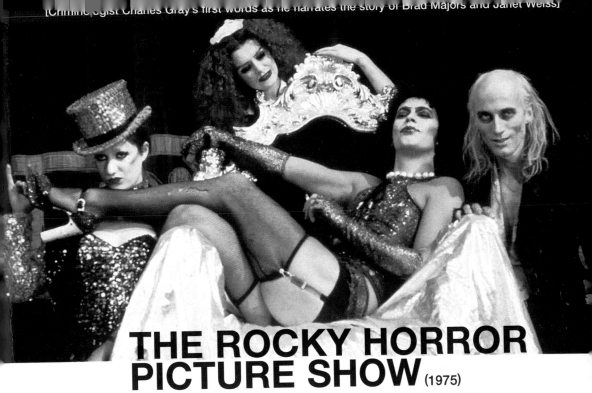

[Chrrmmc egist Charles Gray's first words as he narrates the story of Brad Majors and Janet Weiss]

THE ROCKY HORROR
PICTURE SHOW (1975)

DIRECTOR: Richard O'Brien
WRITERS: Richard O'Brien and Jim Sharman
Dr FRANK-N-FURTER: Tim Curry
JANET WEISS: Susan Sarandon
BRAD MAJORS: Barry Bostwick
ROCKY: Peter Hinwood

[Dr Frank-N-Furter to Brad and
Janet after having them stripped]

And what charming
underclothes you both have.

Scott: I was thinking I like animals. Maybe I'd be a vet.

Dr Evil: An evil vet?

Scott: No! Maybe like work in a petting zoo.

Dr Evil: An evil petting zoo?

Scott: You always do that!

Dr Evil: Scott, I want you to meet
Daddy's nemesis, Austin Powers.

Scott: What? Are you feeding him?
Why don't you just kill him?

Dr Evil: I have an even better idea. I'm going
to place him in an easily escapable situation
involving an overly elaborate and exotic death.

DIRECTOR: Jay Roach
WRITER: Mike Myers
AUSTIN POWERS/DR EVIL: Mike Myers
VANESSA KENSINGTON: Liz Hurley
BASIL EXPOSITION: Michael York
SCOTT EVIL: Seth Green

AUSTIN POWERS:
INTERNATIONAL MAN

[Frozen since the 1960s, awakes in the 1990s]

Austin: As long as people are still having premarital sex with many anonymous partners while at the same time experimenting with mind-expanding drugs in a consequence-free environment, I'll be sound as a pound!

OF MYSTERY (1997)

Han Solo: Hokey religions and ancient weapons are no match for a good blaster at your side, kid.

STAR WARS (1977)

DIRECTOR: George Lucas
WRITER: George Lucas
LUKE SKYWALKER: Mark Hammill
HAN SOLO: Harrison Ford
PRINCESS LEIA ORGANA: Carrie Fisher
BEN (OBI-WAN) KENOBI: Alec Guinness
DARTH VADER: Dave Prowse

Luke: How did my father die?

Obi-Wan: A young Jedi named Darth Vader, who was a pupil of mine until he turned to evil, helped the Empire hunt down and destroy the Jedi knights. He betrayed and murdered your father.

Ben (Obi-Wan) Kenobi: That's no moon. It's a space station.

Han Solo: Look, Your Worshipfulness, let's get one thing straight. I take orders from just one person: me!

Princess Leia: It's a wonder you're still alive. [Pushing past Chewbacca] Will someone get this big walking carpet out of my way?

Darth Vader: The Force is strong with this one.

THE UNTOUCHABLES (1987)

DIRECTOR: Brian De Palma
WRITER: David Mamet
ELIOT NESS: Kevin Costner
JIM MALONE: Sean Connery
GEORGE STONE: Andy Garcia
AL CAPONE: Robert De Niro

MALONE [to Eliot Ness]: You wanna get Capone? Here's how you get him. He pulls a knife, you pull a gun. He sends one of yours to the hospital, you send one of his to the morgue. That's the Chicago way, and that's how you get Capone!

Malone: Just like a wop to bring a knife to a gunfight.

Dr No (1962)

DIRECTOR: Terence Young
WRITERS: Richard Maibaum, Johanna Harwood
    and Berkely Mather, from the novel by Ian Fleming
JAMES BOND: Sean Connery
HONEY RYDER: Ursula Andress
DR NO: Joseph Wiseman
MISS MONEYPENNY: Lois Maxwell

Dr No: The Americans are fools. I offered my services. They refused. So did the East. Now they can both pay for their mistake.

Bond: World domination. The same old dream. Our asylums are full of people who think they're Napoleon. Or God.

James Bond: Moneypenny! What gives?

Miss Moneypenny: Me, given an ounce of encouragement.

CLUELESS (1995)

DIRECTOR: Amy Heckerling
WRITER: Amy Heckerling
CHER HOROWITZ: Alicia Silverstone
DIONNE: Stacey Dash
JOSH: Paul Rudd
MEL: Dan Hedaya

Mel: What the hell is that?

Cher: A dress.

Mel: Says who?

Cher: Calvin Klein.

Mel: So, what did you do in school today?

Cher: Well, I broke in my purple clogs.

Cher: Would you say I'm selfish?

Dionne: No, not to your face.

Murray: Woman, lend me fi' dollas.

Dionne: Murray, I have asked you repeatedly not to call me 'woman'.

Murray: Excuse me, 'Ms. Dionne'.

Dionne: Thank you.

Murray: My street slang is an increasingly valid form of expression. Most of the feminine pronouns do have mocking, but not necessarily misogynistic, undertones.

Cher: I want to do something for humanity.

Josh: How about sterilization?

THE BIG SLEEP (1946)

DIRECTOR: Howard Hawks
WRITERS: William Faulkner, Leigh Brackett and
   Jules Furthman, from the novel by Raymond Chandler
PHILIP MARLOWE: Humphrey Bogart
VIVIAN STERNWOOD RUTLEDGE: Lauren Bacall

Marlowe [to Vivian]: Look angel, I'm tired. My jaw hurts and my ribs ache. I killed a man back there and I had to stand by while a harmless little guy was killed.

Marlowe: What's wrong with you?

Vivian: Nothing you can't fix.

[Vivian to Marlowe, after waiting for him for a long time outside his office]

Vivian: So you do get up. I was beginning to think perhaps you worked in bed, like Marcel Proust.

[Marlowe, comparing Vivian to a horse]

Marlowe: You've got a touch of class, but, uh, I don't know how far you can go.

Vivian: A lot depends on who's in the saddle.

DIRECTOR: Rob Reiner
WRITERS: Christopher Guest, Michael McKean, Harry Shearer and Rob Reiner
MARTY DI BERGI: Rob Reiner
MICK SHRIMPTON: R.J. Parnell
DAVID St HUBBINS: Michael McKean
NIGEL TUFNEL: Christopher Guest

[Reading a review of Spinal Tap's latest album]
Marty Di Bergi: 'This pretentious ponderous collection of religious rock psalms is enough to prompt the question, "What day did the Lord create Spinal Tap, and couldn't he have rested on that day too?"'

[Nigel is playing a soft piece on the piano]

Marty Di Bergi: It's very pretty.

Nigel Tufnel: You know, just simple lines intertwining, you know, very much like –
I'm really influenced by Mozart and Bach, and it's sort of in between those, really. It's like a Mach piece, really. It's sort of –

Marty Di Bergi: What do you call this?

Nigel Tufnel: Well, this piece is called 'Lick My Love Pump'.

David St Hubbins [to Marty Di Bergi]: I'm sure I'd feel much worse if I weren't under such heavy sedation.

Mick Shrimpton: As long as there's, you know, sex and drugs, I can do without the rock 'n' roll.

BARTON FINK (1991)

DIRECTOR: Joel Coen
WRITERS: Ethan and Joel Coen
BARTON FINK: John Turturro
CHARLIE MEADOWS: John Goodman
DETECTIVE MASTRIONOTTI: Richard Portnow
DETECTIVE DEUTSCH: Christopher Murney

Mastrionotti: What do you do, Fink?

Barton: I write.

Deutsch: Oh yeah? What kind of write?

Barton: Well, as a matter of fact I write for the pictures.

Mastrionotti: Big fuckin' deal.

Deutsch: You want my partner to kiss your ass?

Barton: No, I – I didn't mean to sound–

Deutsch: What did you mean?

Barton: I – I've got respect for – for working guys, like you–

Mastrionotti: Jesus! Ain't that a load off!

Barton Fink [to Charlie Meadows]: The life of the mind. There's no road map for that territory. Exploring it can be painful. I have a pain most people don't know anything about.

THE GRADUATE (1967)

DIRECTOR: Mike Nichols
WRITERS: Calder Willingham and Buck Henry, from the novel by Charles Webb
MRS ROBINSON: Anne Bancroft
BENJAMIN BRADDOCK: Dustin Hoffman
ELAINE ROBINSON: Katharine Ross
MR BRADDOCK: William Daniels

Benjamin Braddock: Oh no, Mrs Robinson, oh no.

Mrs Robinson: What's wrong?

Benjamin Braddock: I mean, you didn't expect...

Mrs Robinson: What?

Benjamin Braddock: I mean you didn't really think I'd do something like that!

Mrs Robinson: Like what?

Benjamin Braddock: What do you think?

Mrs Robinson: Well, I don't know.

Benjamin Braddock: For God's sake, Mrs Robinson, here we are, you got me into your house, you give me a drink, you... put on music, now you start opening up your personal life to me and tell me your husband won't be home for hours...

Mrs Robinson: So?

Benjamin Braddock: Mrs Robinson, you're trying to seduce me... aren't you?

[on Ben's plans to marry Elaine Robinson]
Mr Braddock: Ben, this whole idea sounds pretty half-baked?
Benjamin Braddock: No, it's not, Dad, it's completely baked.

Benjamin Braddock: Mrs Robinson, I can't do this. It's all terribly wrong.

Mrs Robinson: Do you find me undesirable?

Benjamin Braddock: Oh no, Mrs Robinson, I think you're the most attractive of all my parents' friends, I mean that.

DIRECTOR: David Fincher
WRITER: Jim Uhls, from the novel by Chuck Palahniuk
TYLER DURDEN: Brad Pitt
NARRATOR: Edward Norton
MARLA SINGER: Helena Bonham Carter

Narrator: Marla was like that cut on the roof of your mouth that would go away if you'd stop tonguing it, but you can't.

Tyler Durden: Our generation has had no Great Depression, no Great War. Our war is spiritual. Our depression is our lives.

Tyler Durden: You are not your job. You are not the money in your bank account. You are not the car you drive. You are not how much money is in your wallet. You are not your fucking khakis. You are the all-singing, all-dancing crap of the world.

Narrator: This is your life and it's ending one minute at a time.

CHINATOWN (1974)

DIRECTOR: Roman Polanski
WRITER: Robert Towne
J.J. (JAKE) GITTES: Jack Nicholson
EVELYN CROSS MULWRAY: Faye Dunaway
NOAH CROSS: John Huston
LIEUTENANT LOU ESCOBAR: Perry Lopez

Escobar: Isn't that your phone number?

Jake Gittes: Is it? I forget. I don't call myself that often.

Noah Cross: 'Course I'm respectable. I'm old. Politicians, ugly buildings, and whores all get respectable if they last long enough.

Duffy [to his boss, Gittes]:

Forget it, Jake, it's Chinatown.

Evelyn Mulwray: Hollis seems to think you're an innocent man.

Jake Gittes: Well, I've been accused of a lot of things before, Mrs Mulwray, but never that.

A HARD DAY'S NIGHT (1964)

DIRECTOR: Richard Lester
WRITER: Alun Owen
JOHN: John Lennon
PAUL: Paul McCartney
GEORGE: George Harrison
RINGO: Ringo Starr
GRANDFATHER: Wilfrid Brambell

Man on train: Don't take that tone with me young man. I fought the war for your sort.

Ringo: I bet you're sorry you won.

Reporter: How did you find America?
John: Turned left at Greenland.

Man on train: I shall call the guard.

Paul: Ah, but what? They don't take kindly to insults you know.

Reporter: What would you call that hairstyle you're wearing?

George: Arthur.

Reporter: Are you a mod, or a rocker?
Ringo: Um, no. I'm a mocker.

BIG NIGHT (1996)

DIRECTORS: Campbell Scott and Stanley Tucci
WRITERS: Joseph Tropiano and Stanley Tucci
PHYLLIS: Minnie Driver
PASCAL: Ian Holm
PRIMO: Tony Shalhoub
SECONDO: Stanley Tucci

Pascal: A guy works all day, he don't want to look at his plate and ask, 'What the fuck is this?' He wants to look at his plate, see a steak, and say, 'I like steak!'

Pascal: Give people what they want, then later you can give them what you want.

Primo: To eat good food is to be close to God

COOL HAND LUKE (1967)

DIRECTOR: Stuart Rosenberg
WRITERS: Donn Pearce and Frank R. Pierson, from the novel by Donn Pearce
LUCAS 'LUKE' JACKSON: Paul Newman
DRAGLINE: George Kennedy

[After Luke wins a game of poker on a bluff]

Dragline: Nothin'. A handful of nothin'. You stupid mother-head. He beat you with nothin'. Just like today when he kept comin' back at me – with nothin'.

Lucas 'Luke' Jackson: Yeah, well, sometimes nothin' can be a real cool hand.

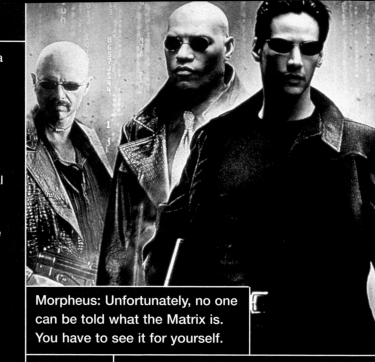

Agent Smith: I'd like to share a revelation that I've had during my time here. It came to me when I tried to classify your species. I realized that you're not actually mammals. Every mammal on this planet instinctively develops a natural equilibrium with the surrounding environment, but you humans do not. You move to an area, and you multiply, and multiply, until every natural resource is consumed. The only way you can survive is to spread to another area. There is another organism on this planet that follows the same pattern. A virus. Human beings are a disease, a cancer of this planet, you are a plague, and we are the cure.

Morpheus: Unfortunately, no one can be told what the Matrix is. You have to see it for yourself.

Morpheus: The Matrix is the world that has been pulled over your eyes to blind you from the truth.

THE MATRIX (1999)

DIRECTORS: The Wachowski Brothers
WRITERS: The Wachowski Brothers
THOMAS A. ANDERSON/NEO: Keanu Reeves
TRINITY: Carrie-Anne Moss
AGENT SMITH: Hugo Weaving
MORPHEUS: Lawrence Fishburne

Neo: What is the Matrix?

Trinity: The answer is out there, Neo, and it's looking for you, and it will find you if you want it to.

SPOON BOY: Do not try and bend the spoon. That's impossible. Instead... only try to realize the truth.

NEO: What truth?

SPOON BOY: There is no spoon.

NEO: There is no spoon?

SPOON BOY: Then you'll see, that it is not the spoon that bends, it is only yourself.

NEO: What are you trying to tell me? That I can dodge bullets?

MORPHEUS: No, Neo. I'm trying to tell you that when you're ready, you won't have to.

Morpheus: Throughout human history, we have been dependent on machines to survive. Fate, it seems, is not without a sense of irony.

Agent Smith: We're willing to wipe the slate clean, give you a fresh start. All that we're asking in return is your co-operation in bringing a known terrorist to justice.

Neo: Yeah. Well, that sounds like a pretty good deal. But I think I may have a better one. How about, I give you the finger... and you give me my phone call.

AGENT SMITH: NEVER SEND A HUMAN TO DO A MACHINE'S JOB.

DIRECTOR: Guy Hamilton
WRITERS: Richard Maibaum and Paul Dehn, from the novel by Ian Fleming
JAMES BOND: Sean Connery
PUSSY GALORE: Honor Blackman
AURIC GOLDFINGER: Gert Fröbe
FELIX LEITER: Cec Linder

Pussy Galore: My name is Pussy Galore.
James Bond: I must be dreaming.

James Bond: Special plane, lunch at the White House... how come?

Felix Leiter: The President wants to thank you personally.

James Bond: Oh, it was nothing, really.

Felix Leiter: I know that, but he doesn't.

James Bond: I suppose I'll be able to get a drink there.

Felix Leiter: I told the stewardess liquor for three.

James Bond: Who are the other two?

Felix Leiter: Oh, there are no other two.

[A laser is about to cut Bond in half.]
James Bond: Do you expect me to talk?
Auric Goldfinger: No, Mr Bond, I expect you to die.

GET CARTER (1971)

DIRECTOR: Mike Hodges
WRITER: Mike Hodges, from the novel by Ted Lewis
JACK CARTER: Michael Caine
ERIC PAICE: Ian Hendry
ANNA FLETCHER: Britt Ekland

Jack Carter: You're a big man, but you're out of shape. With me it's a full time job. Now behave yourself.

Jack Carter: You know, I'd almost forgotten what your eyes looked like. Still the same. Pissholes in the snow.

ALIENS (1986)

DIRECTOR: James Cameron
WRITER: James Cameron
ELLEN RIPLEY: Sigourney Weaver
REBECCA 'NEWT' JORDAN: Carrie Henn
CORPORAL DWAYNE HICKS: Michael Biehn
L. BISHOP: Lance Henriksen
PRIVATE W. HUDSON: Bill Paxton

Newt: We'd better get back, 'cause it'll be dark soon, and they mostly come at night … mostly.

Newt: My mommy always said there were no monsters – no real ones – but there are.

[Lieutenant Gorman orders the troops to unload all their weapons before the first alien encounter.]

Frost: What the hell are we supposed to use, man? Harsh language?

Bishop: I may be synthetic, but I'm not stupid.

LOCK, STOCK AND
TWO SMOKING BARRELS (1998)

DIRECTOR: Guy Ritchie
WRITER: Guy Ritchie
TOM: Jason Flemyng
SOAP: Dexter Fletcher
EDDY: Nick Moran
BACON: Jason Statham

Nick the Greek: I'll need a sample.

Tom: Ahh, no can do I'm afraid.

Nick the Greek: What's that?
Some place near Katmandu?
Meet me halfway mate.

Eddy: There's no money, there's no weed. It's all
been replaced by a fucking big pile of corpses.

Eddy: They're armed.

Soap: Armed? Armed with what?

Eddy: Feather duster, colourful
language, what do you
think? Guns, you tit!

Big Chris: It's been emotional.

Rory Breaker:
If you hold
back anything,
I'll kill ya.
If you bend the
truth or I think
your bending
the truth,
I'll kill ya.
If you forget
anything
I'll kill ya.
In fact, you're
gonna have
to work very
hard to stay
alive, Nick.
Now do you
understand
everything I've
said? Because
if you don't,
I'll kill ya.

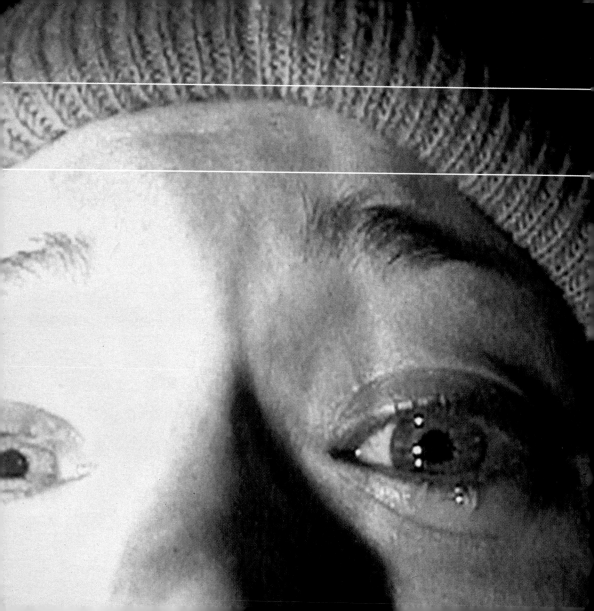

THE BLAIR WITCH PROJECT (1999)

DIRECTORS: Daniel Myrick and Eduardo Sánchez

WRITERS: Daniel Myrick and Eduardo Sánchez

HEATHER DONAHUE: Heather Donahue

MICHAEL WILLIAMS: Michael Williams

JOSH LEONARD: Joshua Leonard

THE ADVENTURES OF PRISCILLA, QUEEN OF THE DESERT (1994)

DIRECTOR: Stephan Elliott
WRITER: Stephan Elliott
TICK/MITZI: Hugo Weaving
ADAM WHITELY/FELICIA: Guy Pearce
BERNARDETTE: Terence Stamp
BOB: Bill Hunter

Bernadette: I'll join this conversation on the proviso that we stop bitching about people, talking about wigs, dresses, bust sizes, penises, drugs, night clubs and bloody Abba!

Tick: Doesn't give us much to talk about then, does it?

Bernadette: Stop flexing your muscles, you big pile of budgie turd. I'm sure your mates will be much more impressed if you just go back to the pub and fuck a couple of pigs on the bar.

Bob: Bernadette, please.

Frank: BERNADETTE? Well I'll be darned. The whole circus is in town. Well I suppose you wanna fuck too, do you? Come on Bernadette, come and fuck me. That's it. Come on. Come and fuck me. Come on.

[Bernadette knees Frank in the groin.]

Bernadette: There, now you're fucked!

Bernadette: Just what this country needs: a cock in a frock on a rock.

GUESS WHO'S COMING TO DINNER (1967)

DIRECTOR: Stanley Kramer
WRITER: William Rose
MATT DRAYTON: Spencer Tracy
JOHN WADE PRENTICE: Sidney Poitier
CHRISTINA DRAYTON: Katharine Hepburn

Matt Drayton: You're two wonderful people who happened to fall in love and happen to have a pigmentation problem.

[Spencer Tracy's last movie line]

Matt Drayton: Well, Tillie, when the hell are we going to get some dinner?

AMERICAN BEAUTY (1999)

DIRECTOR: Sam Mendes
WRITER: Alan Ball
LESTER BURNHAM: Kevin Spacey
CAROLYN BURNHAM: Annette Bening
JANE BURNHAM: Thora Birch
RICKY FITTS: Wes Bentley
ANGELA HAYES: Mena Suvari

[Reading Lester's job description]
Brad: 'My job requires mostly masking my contempt for the assholes in charge, and, at least once a day, retiring to the men's room so I can jerk off while I fantasize about a life that doesn't so closely resemble Hell.'

Ricky Fitts: It was one of those days when it's a minute away from snowing and there's this electricity in the air, you can almost hear it, right? And this bag was like, dancing with me. Like a little kid begging me to play with it. For fifteen minutes. And that's the day I knew there was this entire life behind things, and... this incredibly benevolent force, that wanted me to know there was no reason to be afraid, ever. Video's a poor excuse. But it helps me remember... and I need to remember... Sometimes there's so much beauty in the world I feel like I can't take it, like my heart's going to cave in.

DIRTY HARRY (1971)

DIRECTOR: Don Siegel
WRITERS: Harry Julian Fink, Rita M. Fink
   and Dean Riesner
HARRY CALLAHAN: Clint Eastwood
BRESSLER: Harry Guardino
CHICO: Reni Santoni

CALLAHAN: I know what you're thinking. Did he fire six shots or only five? Well, to tell you the truth, in all this excitement, I've kinda lost track myself. But being as this is a .44 Magnum, the most powerful handgun in the world, and would blow your head clean off, you've got to ask yourself one question: 'Do I feel lucky?' Well, do ya, punk?

BREAKFAST AT TIFFANY'S (1961)

DIRECTOR: Blake Edwards

WRITER: George Axelrod, from the novel by Truman Capote

HOLLY GOLIGHTLY: Audrey Hepburn

PAUL VARJAK: George Peppard

Holly: He's alright! Aren't you, cat? Poor cat! Poor slob! Poor slob without a name! The way I see it I haven't got the right to give him one. We don't belong to each other. We just took up one day by the river. I don't want to own anything until I find a place where me and things go together. I'm not sure where that is but I know what it is like. It's like Tiffany's.

Paul: Tiffany's? You mean the jewellery store.

Holly: That's right. I'm just CRAZY about Tiffany's!

Holly: You know those days when you get the mean reds?

Paul: The mean reds, you mean like the blues?

Holly: No. The blues are because you're getting fat or maybe it's been raining too long, you're just sad, that's all. The mean reds are horrible. Suddenly you're afraid and you don't know what you're afraid of. Do you ever get that feeling?

Paul: Sure.

Holly: Well, when I get it the only thing that does any good is to jump into a cab and go to Tiffany's. Calms me down right away.

Paul: You know what's wrong with you, Miss Whoever-you-are? You're chicken, you've got no guts. You're afraid to stick out your chin and say, 'Okay, life's a fact, people do fall in love, people do belong to each other, because that's the only chance anybody's got for real happiness.' You call yourself a free spirit, a 'wild thing', and you're terrified somebody's gonna stick you in a cage. Well baby, you're already in that cage. You built it yourself. And it's not bounded in the west by Tulip, Texas, or in the east by Somaliland. It's wherever you go. Because no matter where you run, you just end up running into yourself.

THE ITALIAN JOB (1969)

DIRECTOR: Peter Collinson
WRITER: Troy Kennedy-Martin
CHARLIE CROKER: Michael Caine
Mr BRIDGER: Noel Coward
PROFESSOR PEACH: Benny Hill

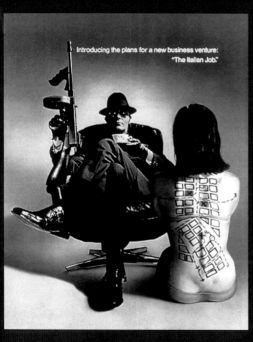

Charlie:
Hang on lads,
I've got a
great idea.

GARAGE MANAGER:
You must have shot an
awful lot of tigers, sir.

CHARLIE:
Yes, I use a machine gun.

[Arthur blows up a truck.]

Charlie: You're only supposed
to blow the bloody doors off!

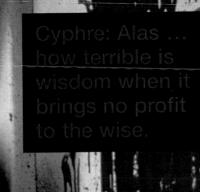

Cyphre: Alas ... how terrible is wisdom when it brings no profit to the wise.

Cyphre: Are you an atheist?

Angel: Yeah, I'm from Brooklyn.

ANGEL HEART (1987)

DIRECTOR: Alan Parker
WRITER: Alan Parker, from the novel by William Hjortsberg
HARRY ANGEL: Mickey Rourke
LOUIS CYPHRE: Robert De Niro

PLANET OF THE APES (1968)

DIRECTOR: Franklin J. Schaffner
WRITERS: Michael Wilson and Rod Serling, based on *Monkey Planet* by Pierre Boulle
COL. GEORGE TAYLOR: Charlton Heston
DR CORNELIUS: Roddy McDowall

Cornelius: We thought you were inferior.
George Taylor: Now you know better.

George Taylor: Get your stinking paws off me, you damned dirty ape!

FLASH GORDON (1980)

DIRECTOR: Mike Hodges
WRITERS: Michael Allin and Lorenzo Semple Jr.,
  from the comic strip by Alex Raymond
FLASH GORDON: Sam Jones
MING THE MERCILESS: Max von Sydow
DALE ARDEN: Melody Anderson

Clytus: Most effective, Your Majesty. Will you destroy this Earth?

Ming the Merciless: Later. I like to play with things a while before annihilation.

Aura: Look! Water is leaking from her eyes.

Ming the Merciless: It's what they call tears, it's a sign of their weakness.

Dale Arden: Flash, Flash, I love you, but we only have fourteen hours to save the Earth!

PULP FICTION (1994)

DIRECTOR: Quentin Tarantino
WRITER: Quentin Tarantino
VINCENT VEGA: John Travolta
JULES WINNFIELD: Samuel L. Jackson
BUTCH COOLIDGE: Bruce Willis

VINCENT: And you know what they call a Quarter Pounder with Cheese in Paris?

JULES: They don't call it a Quarter Pounder with Cheese?

VINCENT: No man, they got the metric system. They wouldn't know what the fuck a Quarter Pounder is.

JULES: Then what do they call it?

VINCENT: They call it a 'Royale' with cheese.

JULES: A 'Royale' with cheese! What do they call a Big Mac?

VINCENT: A Big Mac's a Big Mac, but they call it 'le Big-Mac'.

JULES: 'Le Big-Mac'! Ha ha ha ha! What do they call a Whopper?

VINCENT: I dunno, I didn't go into Burger King.

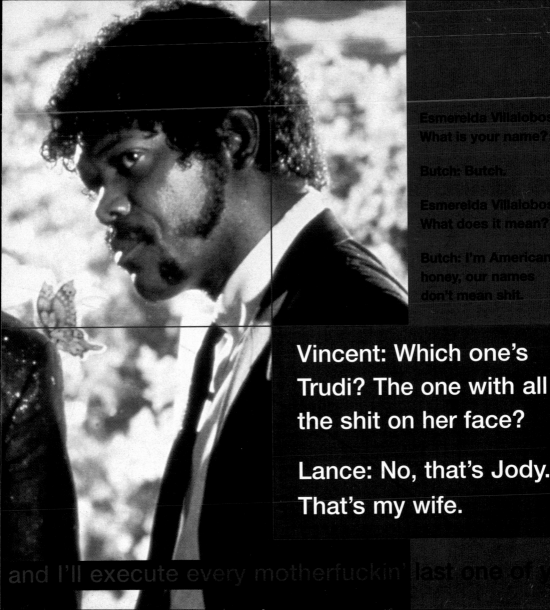

Esmerelda Villalobos:
What is your name?

Butch: Butch.

Esmerelda Villalobos:
What does it mean?

Butch: I'm American,
honey, our names
don't mean shit.

Vincent: Which one's
Trudi? The one with all
the shit on her face?

Lance: No, that's Jody.
That's my wife.

and I'll execute every motherfuckin' last one of

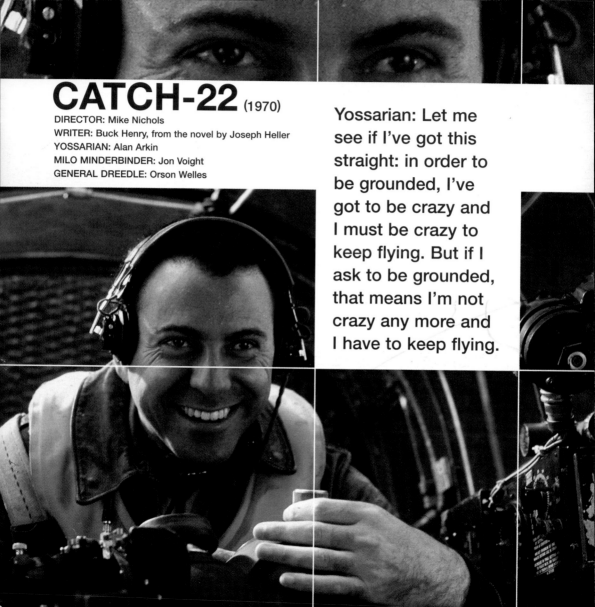

CATCH-22 (1970)

DIRECTOR: Mike Nichols
WRITER: Buck Henry, from the novel by Joseph Heller
YOSSARIAN: Alan Arkin
MILO MINDERBINDER: Jon Voight
GENERAL DREEDLE: Orson Welles

Yossarian: Let me see if I've got this straight: in order to be grounded, I've got to be crazy and I must be crazy to keep flying. But if I ask to be grounded, that means I'm not crazy any more and I have to keep flying.

BEING JOHN MALKOVICH (1999)

John Horatio Malkovich: You see, Maxine, it isn't just playing with dolls.

Maxine: You're right, my darling, it's so much more. It's playing with people!

DIRECTOR: Spike Jonze
WRITER: Charlie Kaufman
CRAIG SCHWARTZ: John Cusack
LOTTE SCHWARTZ: Cameron Diaz
MAXINE: Catherine Keener
JOHN HORATIO MALKOVICH: John Malkovich

Craig Schwartz: With all due respect, John, It's MY portal.
John Horatio Malkovich: It's MY HEAD, Schwartz. It's MY head!

BLADE RUNNER (1982)

DIRECTOR: Ridley Scott
WRITERS: Hampton Fancher and David Peoples, from the novel by Philip K. Dick
RICK DECKARD: Harrison Ford
ROY BATTY: Rutger Hauer
RACHAEL: Sean Young

Tyrell: 'More human than human' is our motto.

Deckard: I have had people walk
out on me before, but not when
I was being so charming.

THE SIXTH SENSE (1999)

DIRECTOR: M. Night Shyamalan
WRITER: M. Night Shyamalan
MALCOLM CROWE: Bruce Willis
COLE SEAR: Joel Haley Osment

Cole Sear: We were supposed to draw a picture, anything we wanted. I drew a man who got hurt in the neck by another man with a screwdriver... everyone got upset. They had a meeting. Mom started crying. I don't draw like that any more.

Malcolm Crowe: How do you draw now?

Cole Sear: People smiling, dogs running, rainbows. They don't have meetings about rainbows.

Cole Sear: I see dead people.

Brian's mother: He's not the Messiah. He's a very naughty boy!

[A line of prisoners files past a jailer.]

Jailer: Crucifixion?

Prisoner: Yes.

Jailer: Good. Out of the door, line on the left, one cross each. [Next prisoner] Crucifixion?

Prisoner 2: Er, no, freedom actually.

Jailer: What?

Prisoner 2: Yeah, they said I hadn't done anything and I could go and live on an island somewhere.

Jailer: Oh I say, that's very nice. Well, off you go then.

Prisoner 2: No, I'm only joking, it's crucifixion really.

Jailer: [laughing] Oh yes, very good. Well...

Prisoner 2: Yes I know, out of the door, one cross each, line on the left.

Reg:
All right, but apart from the sanitation, medicine, education, wine, public order, irrigation, roads, the fresh water system and public health, what have the Romans ever done for us?

Attendee:
Brought peace?

Reg:
Oh, peace – shut up!

THE LIFE OF BRIAN (1979)

DIRECTOR: Terry Jones
WRITERS: Graham Chapman, John Cleese, Terry Gilliam,
   Eric Idle, Terry Jones and Michael Palin
BRIAN/VARIOUS: Graham Chapman
BRIAN'S MOTHER/VARIOUS: Terry Jones
REG/VARIOUS: John Cleese

Brian: I'm not a Roman, Mum, I'm a kike, a yid, a heebie, a hook-nose, I'm kosher Mum, I'm a Red Sea pedestrian, and proud of it!

Brian:
You are all individuals!

The Crowd:
We are all individuals!

Brian:
You have to be different!

The Crowd:
Yes, we are all different!

Small lonely voice:
I'm not different!

Wise man:
We were led by a star.

Brian's mother:
Led by a bottle, you mean.

WHEN HARRY MET SALLY (1989)

DIRECTOR: Rob Reiner
WRITER: Nora Ephron
HARRY BURNS: Billy Crystal
SALLY ALBRIGHT: Meg Ryan

Sally [lamenting old age]:
I'm gonna be forty.

Harry: When?

Sally: Someday.

Harry: No man can be friends with a woman
that he finds attractive. He always wants
to have sex with her.

Sally: So you're saying that a man can be friends
with a woman he finds unattractive.

Harry: No, you pretty much want to nail them too.

Sally [to Harry]: Most women at one time or another have faked it.

How
did they
ever
make
a film
of

LOLITA
?

X ADULTS ONLY

METRO-GOLDWYN-MAYER presents in association with SEVEN ARTS PRODUCTIONS JAMES B. HARRIS and STANLEY KUBRICK's **LOLITA**

JAMES MASON · SHELLEY WINTERS · PETER SELLERS **SUE LYON**

Screenplay by VLADIMIR NABOKOV · Directed by STANLEY KUBRICK · Produced by JAMES B. HARRIS

LOLITA (1962)

DIRECTOR: Stanley Kubrick
WRITER: Vladimir Nabokov
HUMBERT HUMBERT: James Mason
CHARLOTTE HAZE: Shelley Winters
LOLITA HAYES: Sue Lyon

Charlotte Haze: Do you believe in God?

Humbert Humbert: The question is does God believe in me?

Charlotte Haze: Whenever you touch me, darling, I go as limp as a noodle

Humbert Humbert: Yes, I am familiar with that feeling

THE BIG CHILL (1983)

DIRECTOR: Lawrence Kasdan
WRITERS: Barbara Benedek and Lawrence Kasdan
SAM WEBER: Tom Berenger
SARAH: Glenn Close
MICHAEL: Jeff Goldblum
MEG: Mary Kay Place
KAREN: Jo Beth Williams

KAREN: I know that Richard will always be faithful to me.

HAROLD: That's nice. Trust.

KAREN: Fear of herpes.

Meg [About men]: They're either married or gay. And if they're not gay, they've just broken up with the most wonderful woman in the world, or they've just broken up with a bitch who looks exactly like me. They're in transition from a monogamous relationship and they need more space. Or they're tired of space, but they just can't commit. Or they want to commit, but they're afraid to get close. They want to get close; you don't want to get near them.

Meg: I'm going to wash my hair and puke.

Michael: Puke first.

TO KILL A MOCKINGBIRD (1962)

DIRECTOR: Robert Mulligan
WRITER: Horton Foote, from the novel by Harper Lee
ATTICUS FINCH: Gregory Peck
TOM ROBINSON: Brock Peters

Atticus Finch: You never really understand a person until you consider things from his point of view...'til you climb inside of his skin and walk around in it.

THE COMMITMENTS (1991)

DIRECTOR: Alan Parker
WRITERS: Dick Clement and Ian La Frenais,
    from the novel by Roddy Doyle
JIMMY RABBITTE: Robert Arkins
DECO CUFFE: Andrew Strong

Jimmy Rabbitte: What do you play?

Punk: I used to play football in school.

Jimmy Rabbitte: I mean what instrument?

Punk: I don't play an instrument.

Jimmy Rabbitte: Then why are you here?

Punk: Well, I saw everyone else lining up so I thought you were selling drugs.

YOU ONLY LIVE TWICE (1967)

DIRECTOR: Lewis Gilbert
WRITER: Roald Dahl, from the novel by Ian Fleming
JAMES BOND: Sean Connery
KISSY SUZUKI: Mie Hama
ERNST STAVRO BLOFELD: Donald Pleasence

Blofeld: James Bond. Allow me to introduce myself. I am Ernst Stavro Blofeld. They told me you were assassinated in Hong Kong.

James Bond: Yes, this is my second life.

Blofeld: You only live twice, Mr Bond.

Cab dispatcher: Why do you want to drive a cab?

Travis: I can't sleep at nights.

Cab dispatcher: There's porno theatres for that.

TAXI DRIVER (1976)

DIRECTOR: Martin Scorcese
WRITER: Paul Schrader
TRAVIS BICKLE: Robert De Niro
IRIS: Jodie Foster

[Into a mirror]
Travis Bickle:
You talkin' to me?
You talkin' to me?
You talkin' to me?
Then who the hell else are you talkin' to?
You talkin' to me?
Well I'm the only one here. Who do you think you're talking to? Oh yeah? Huh? OK.

Travis Bickle: I think someone should just take this city and just... just flush it down the fuckin' toilet.

THE BREAKFAST CLUB (1985)

DIRECTOR: John Hughes
WRITER: John Hughes
ANDREW CLARK: Emilio Estevez
CLAIRE STANDISH: Molly Ringwald
ALLISON REYNOLDS: Ally Sheedy
BRIAN JOHNSON: Anthony Michael Hall
JOHN BENDER: Judd Nelson

Brian: Dear Mr Vernon, we accept the fact that we had to sacrifice a whole Saturday in detention for whatever it is we did wrong, but we think you're crazy for making us write an essay telling you who we think we are. You see us as you want to see us: in the simplest terms, and in the most convenient definitions. But what we found out is that each one of us is a brain, and an athlete, and a basket case, and a princess, and a criminal. Does that answer your question? Sincerely yours, The Breakfast Club.

Allison: Your middle name is Ralph, as in puke, your birthday's March 12th, you're five feet nine and a half, you weigh 130 pounds and your social security number is 049380913.

Andrew: Wow! Are you psychic?

Allison: No.

Brian: Well, would you mind telling me how you know all this about me?

Allison: I stole your wallet.

CLAIRE: He's just doing it to get a rise out of you. Just ignore him.

JOHN: Sweets, you couldn't ignore me if you tried. So… so. Are you guys like boyfriend-girlfriend? Steady dates? Lovers? Come on, sporto, level with me. Do you slip her the hot beef injection?

AS GOOD AS IT GETS (1997)

DIRECTOR: James L. Brooks
WRITERS: Mark Andrus and James L. Brooks
MELVIN UDALL: Jack Nicholson
CAROL CONNELLY: Helen Hunt
SIMON BISHOP: Greg Kinnear

MELVIN: Never, never, interrupt me, OK? Not if there's a fire, not even if you can hear the sound of a thud from my home and one week later there's a smell coming from there that can only be a decaying human body and you have to hold a hanky to your face because the stench is so thick that you think you're going to faint. Even then, don't come knocking. Or, if it's election night, and you're excited and you wanna celebrate because some fudgepacker that you date has been elected the first queer President of the United States and he's going to have you down to Camp David, and you want someone to share the moment with. Even then, don't knock. Not on this door. Not for ANY reason. Do you get me, sweetheart?

SIMON: It's not a subtle point that you're making.

RESERVOIR DOGS (1992)

DIRECTOR: Quentin Tarantino
WRITER: Quentin Tarantino
Mʀ WHITE/LARRY: Harvey Keitel
FREDDY NEWENDYKE/Mʀ ORANGE: Tim Roth
VIC VEGA/Mʀ BLONDE: Michael Madsen
NICE GUY EDDIE: Chris Penn
Mʀ PINK: Steve Buscemi
JOE CABOT: Lawrence Tierney

Mr Brown: Mr Brown? That sounds too much like Mr Shit.

Joe Cabot: And you are Mr Pink.
Mr Pink: Why am I Mr Pink?
Joe Cabot: 'Cause you're a faggot, OK?

Mr Pink: You kill anybody?
Mr White: A few cops.
Mr Pink: No real people?
Mr White: Just cops.

Joe Cabot: Let's go to work.

BILL AND TED'S
EXCELLENT ADVENTURE (1989)

DIRECTOR: Stephen Herek
WRITERS: Chris Matheson and Ed Solomon
THEODORE 'TED' LOGAN: Keanu Reeves
BILL S. PRESTON: Alex Winter
MR RYAN: Bernie Casey

[Bill and Ted are working on their history report.]

BILL: George Washington: the father of our country.

TED: Also born on President's Day.

BILL: The dollar bill guy.

TED: Hey, did you ever make a mushroom out of his head–?

BILL: Ted?

TED: What?

BILL: Alaska.

TED: Oh yeah. [Thinks for a moment] Had wooden teeth, chased Moby Dick!

BILL: That's Captain Ahab, dude.

History teacher:
Who was Joan of Arc?

Ted: Noah's wife?

Mr Ryan: All you boys seem to have learned is that Caesar is a 'salad dressing dude'.

AUSTIN POWERS:
THE SPY WHO SHAGGED ME (1999)

DIRECTOR: Jay Roach
WRITERS: Mike Myers and Michael McCullers
AUSTIN POWERS/DR EVIL/FAT BASTARD: Mike Myers
FELICITY SHAGWELL: Heather Graham

Austin: I put the 'grrrrr' in swinger, baby, yeah!

DR EVIL [to Scott Evil]: You're not quite evil enough. You're semi-evil. You're quasi-evil. You're the margarine of evil. You're the Diet Coke of evil, just one calorie, not evil enough.

Felicity: Felicity Shagwell. Shagwell by name, shag-very-well by reputation.

AUSTIN: [About Felicity's skin-tight clothes] How do you get into those pants?

FELICITY: Well, you can start by buying me a drink.

THE ADVENTURES OF
BARON MUNCHAUSEN (1988)

DIRECTOR: Terry Gilliam
WRITERS: Terry Gilliam and Charles McKeown, from the novel by Rudolph Erich Raspe
BARON MUNCHAUSEN: John Neville
DESMOND/BERTHOLD: Eric Idle
VULCAN: Oliver Reed

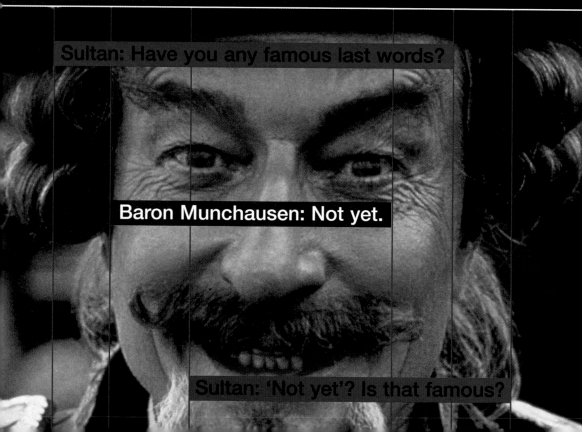

Sultan: Have you any famous last words?

Baron Munchausen: Not yet.

Sultan: 'Not yet'? Is that famous?

AMERICAN PIE (1999)

DIRECTOR: Paul Weitz
WRITER: Adam Herz
JIM: Jason Biggs
CHRIS 'OZ' OSTREICHER: Chris Klein
MICHELLE: Alyson Hannigan
KEVIN: Thomas Ian Nicholas
JIM'S DAD: Eugene Levy

Jim: Guys, uh, what exactly does third base feel like?

Kevin [to Chris]: You want to take this one?

Chris: Like warm apple pie.

Jim: Yeah?

Chris: Yeah.

Jim: Apple pie, huh?

Chris: Uh huh.

Jim: McDonald's or homemade?

Jim's Dad: I have to admit, you know, I did a fair bit of [hesitates] masturbating when I was a little younger. I used to call it stroking the salami, yeah, you know, pounding the old pud. [Pause] I never did it with baked goods, but you know your uncle Mort, he pets the one-eyed snake 5–6 times a day.

Michelle: One time, at band camp, I put my flute up my pussy. What, you don't think I know how to get myself off?

Bonnie Parker: [reading her poem]

You've heard the story of Jesse James

Of how he lived and died

If you're still in need

Of something to read

Here's the story of Bonnie and Clyde.

Now Bonnie and Clyde are the Barrow gang

I'm sure you all have read

How they rob and steal

And those who squeal

Are usually found dyin' or dead.

They call them cold-hearted killers

They say they are heartless and mean

But I say this with pride

That I once knew Clyde

When he was honest and upright and clean.

But the laws fooled around

Kept takin' him down

And lockin' him up in a cell

Till he said to me: 'I'll never be free

So I'll meet a few of them in Hell.'

If a policeman is killed in Dallas

And they have no clue to guide

If they can't find a fiend

They just wipe their slate clean

And hang it on Bonnie and Clyde.

If they try to act like citizens

And rent them a nice little flat

About the third night

They're invited to fight

By a sub-gun's rat-a-tat-tat.

Some day, they'll go down together

They'll bury them side by side

To a few, it'll be grief

To the law, a relief

But it's death for Bonnie and Clyde.

BONNIE AND CLYDE (1967)

DIRECTOR: Arthur Penn
WRITERS: David Newman and Robert Benton
CLYDE BARROW: Warren Beatty
BONNIE PARKER: Faye Dunaway

STAR WARS EPISODE 1 –
THE PHANTOM MENACE (1999)

DIRECTOR: George Lucas
WRITER: George Lucas
QUI-GON JINN: Liam Neeson
OBI-WAN KENOBI: Ewan McGregor
QUEEN AMIDALA: Natalie Portman
ANAKIN SKYWALKER: Jake Lloyd

Watto: How are you going to pay for all this?

Qui-Gon: I have twenty thousand Republic dataries.

Watto: Republic credits? Republic credits are no good out here. I need something more real.

Qui-Gon: I don't have have anything else [waves hand] but credits will do fine.

Watto: No, they won't-a.

[Qui-Gon waves his hand more firmly.]

Qui-Gon: Credits will do fine.

Watto: No, they won't-a. What? You think you're some kind of Jedi, waving your hand around like that? I'm a Toydarian, mind tricks don't work on me. Only money. No money, no parts, no deal!

YODA: [to Anakin] Fear is the path to the dark side. Fear leads to anger. Anger leads to hate. Hate leads to suffering. I sense much fear in you.

WITHNAIL & I (1987)

DIRECTOR: Bruce Robinson
WRITER: Bruce Robinson
WITHNAIL: Richard E. Grant
PETER MARWOOD: Paul McGann
MONTY: Richard Griffiths
DANNY: Ralph Brown

[talking about his very long spliff]
Danny: It is called a Camberwell Carrot because I invented it in Camberwell and it looks like a carrot.

Withnail: We've come on holiday by mistake.

DANNY: I don't advise a haircut, man. All hairdressers are in the employment of the government. Hairs are your aerials. They pick up signals from the cosmos, and transmit them directly into the brain. This is the reason bald-headed men are uptight.

Monty: I mean to have you, boy, even if it must be burglary.

Withnail: I feel like a pig shat in my head.

Withnail: I demand to have some booze!

THE BIG LEBOWSKI (1998)

DIRECTOR: Joel Coen
WRITERS: Ethan and Joel Coen
THE DUDE: Jeff Bridges
WALTER SOBCHAK: John Goodman
MAUDE LEBOWSKI: Julianne Moore
JESUS QUINTANA: John Turturro

Walter: My point is, here we are, it's shabbas, the sabbath, which I'm allowed to break only if it's a matter of life or death–

Dude: Will you come off it, Walter? You're not even fucking Jewish, man.

Walter: What the fuck are you talkin' about?

Dude: Man, you're fucking Polish Catholic–

Walter: What the fuck are you talking about? I converted when I married Cynthia! Come on, Dude!

Dude: Yeah, yeah, yeah, yeah–

Walter: And you know this!

Dude: Yeah, and five fucking years ago you were divorced.

Walter: So what are you saying? When you get divorced you turn in your library card? You get a new license? You stop being Jewish?

Dude: It's all a part of your sick Cynthia thing, man. Taking care of her fucking dog. Going to her fucking synagogue. You're living in the fucking past.

Walter: Three thousand years of beautiful tradition, from Moses to Sandy Koufax – YOU'RE GODDAMN RIGHT I'M LIVING IN THE FUCKING PAST!

Walter: This is not 'Nam. This is bowling. There are rules.

JESUS: You ready to be fucked, man?
I see you rolled your way into the semis.
Dios mio, man. Seamus and me, we're
gonna fuck you up.

DUDE: Yeah, well, that's just, like, your
opinion, man.

JESUS: Let me tell you something, *pendejo*.
You pull any of your crazy shit with us, you
flash a piece out on the lanes, I'll take it
away from you, stick it up your ass and
pull the fucking trigger 'til it goes 'click'.

DUDE: Jesus.

JESUS: You said it, man. Nobody fucks
with the Jesus.

DUDE: Nobody calls me Lebowski. You got
    the wrong guy. I'm the Dude, man.
TREEHORN'S THUG: Your name's Lebowski,
    Lebowski. Your wife is Bunny.
DUDE: My... my wi– my wife, Bunny?
    Do you see a wedding ring on my finger?
    Does this place look like I'm fucking
    married? The toilet seat's up, man!

AMADEUS (1984)

DIRECTOR: Milos Forman
WRITER: Peter Shaffer
ANTONIO SALIERI: F. Murray Abraham
WOLFGANG AMADEUS MOZART: Tom Hulce
EMPEROR JOSEPH II: Jeffrey Jones

Salieri: God was singing through this little man to all the world, making my defeat more bitter with every passing bar.

EMPEROR: Your work is ingenious. It's quality work. But there are simply too many notes, that's all. Just cut a few and it will be perfect.

MOZART: Which few did you have in mind, Majesty?

Mozart: Forgive me, Your Majesty. I am a vulgar man. But my music is not.

DIRECTOR: John Hughes
WRITER: John Hughes
FERRIS BUELLER: Matthew Broderick
CAMERON FRYE: Alan Ruck
SLOANE PETERSON: Mia Sara

Ferris: I did have a test today. That wasn't bullshit. It's on European Socialism. I mean, really, what's the point? I'm not European, I don't plan on being European, so who gives a crap if they're socialist? They could be fascist anarchists, that still wouldn't change the fact that I don't own a car. Not that I condone fascism, or any 'ism' for that matter. 'Isms' in my opinion are not good. A person should not believe in an 'ism', he should believe in himself. I quote John Lennon: 'I don't believe in the Beatles, I just believe in me.' A good point there. Of course he was the walrus. I could be the walrus, I'd still have to bum rides off of people.

Ferris: Life moves pretty fast. If you don't stop and look around once in a while, you could miss it.

JAWS (1975)

DIRECTOR: Steven Spielberg
WRITERS: Peter Benchley and Carl Gottlieb
MARTIN BRODY: Roy Scheider
QUINT: Robert Shaw
MATT HOOPER: Richard Dreyfuss
MAYOR LARRY VAUGHN: Murray Hamilton

Mayor Vaughn: Martin, it's all psychological. You yell barracuda, everybody says, 'Huh? What?' You yell shark, we've got a panic on our hands on the Fourth of July.

Hooper: Mr. Vaughn, what we are dealing with here is a perfect engine, er... an eating machine. It's really a miracle of evolution. All this machine does is swim and eat and make little sharks and that's all.

Mayor Vaughn: I don't think either of you are familiar with our problems.

Hooper: I am familiar with the fact that you are going to ignore this particluar problem until it swims up and bites you on the ass!

Hooper: This was no boat accident!

Hooper: I'm not going to waste my time arguing with a man who's lining up to be a hot lunch.